NURTURING YOU: A SELF-CARE GUIDE FOR WOMEN

JENNIFER L. BALDWIN

ABOUT THE AUTHOR

Jennifer L. Baldwin, is a passionate advocate for self-love and personal growth. With a deep commitment to helping others discover their true worth and potential, Jennifer Baldwin has dedicated her life to empowering individuals to lead more fulfilling and authentic lives. Through her work as a best-selling author and Master life coach, Jennifer Baldwin has inspired countless people to embark on the transformative journey of self-love. Jennifer Baldwin envisions a world where self-love is the foundation of personal and collective well-being. She is dedicated to continuing her mission of spreading awareness and education about the importance of self-love. Through her writings, speaking engagements, and coaching, Jennifer Baldwin aims to inspire and empower more individuals to embark on the journey of self-love and create positive, lasting change in their lives. To contact the author, visit www.jennbaldwin.com.

Copyright © 2024 Jennifer Baldwin

All rights reserved. No part of this publication may be reproduced, distributed, or transmitted in any form or by any means without the prior written permission of the publisher, except in the case of brief quotations embodied in articles and reviews.

ISBN: 979-8-3304-2973-8
Cover Designed and Published by JR Publishing, 2024

Dedication

To every woman who has ever felt overwhelmed, undervalued, or unseen—This book is for you.

May you find the courage to prioritize your own well-being, the strength to embrace your imperfections, and the grace to love yourself fully.

You are worthy of all the love, care, and joy this world has to offer. May this guide be a gentle reminder that nurturing yourself is not just a gift to you, but a gift to everyone around you.

With love and light,

Jennifer L. Baldwin

Table of Contents

Introduction 1

Mindfulness and Meditation 4

Physical Well-Being 9

Emotional Health 16

Creative Outlets 23

Social Connections 29

Self-Love and Acceptance 35

Final Thoughts 41

Introduction

Welcome to **Nurturing You: A Self-Care Guide for Women**. In the fast-paced world we live in, it's all too easy for women to find themselves juggling multiple responsibilities, often prioritizing the needs of others over their own. This guide is designed to help you shift that balance, placing your well-being at the forefront.

Self-care is not a luxury; it's a necessity. It is the foundation upon which you build a fulfilling and balanced life. When you take the time to nurture yourself, you become better equipped to handle life's challenges, support those around you, and pursue your dreams with vitality and joy.

This book is a comprehensive resource that addresses various aspects of self-care, from mindfulness and meditation to physical well-being, emotional health, creative outlets, social connections, and the all-important practice of self-love and acceptance. Each chapter provides practical tips, reflective exercises, and inspirational sayings to support you on your journey.

- **Mindfulness and Meditation**: Learn to cultivate inner peace and present-moment awareness through simple yet powerful practices.
- **Physical Well-being**: Discover ways to nourish and care for your body, embracing a holistic approach to health.
- **Emotional Health**: Explore strategies to manage stress, process emotions, and foster a resilient mindset.
- **Creative Outlets**: Unleash your creativity as a form of self-expression and relaxation.
- **Social Connections**: Understand the importance of nurturing relationships and building a supportive community.
- **Self-Love and Acceptance**: Embrace who you are, celebrate your uniqueness, and cultivate a loving relationship with yourself.

Throughout the book, you will find encouragement to prioritize your needs, set healthy boundaries, and create rituals that rejuvenate your mind, body, and spirit. Whether you are new to self-care or looking to deepen your existing practices, this guide offers valuable insights and tools to help you thrive.

Embark on this journey of self-discovery and empowerment. Take each step with compassion and patience, knowing that the effort you invest in yourself is the greatest gift you can give. Remember, you are deserving of all the love, care, and happiness that life has to offer.

Welcome to a path of nurturing, growth, and profound self-care. Welcome to **Nurturing You**.

Chapter 1: Mindfulness and Meditation

Introduction to Mindfulness

Mindfulness is the practice of being fully present in the moment, aware of where we are and what we're doing, without being overly reactive or overwhelmed by what's going on around us. It's about slowing down, paying attention to our thoughts, feelings, and sensations, and finding a sense of peace and clarity in the present moment.

Benefits of Mindfulness:

- Reduces stress and anxiety
- Improves focus and concentration
- Enhances emotional regulation
- Promotes a sense of well-being and happiness

Getting Started with Mindfulness:

- **Find a Quiet Space:** Choose a calm and comfortable spot where you can sit undisturbed for a few minutes.

- **Set a Timer:** Start with just 5 minutes a day, gradually increasing the time as you become more comfortable.
- **Focus on Your Breath:** Pay attention to your breathing. Notice the sensation of the air entering and leaving your body.

Meditation Practices

Meditation is a powerful tool to cultivate mindfulness and bring about a sense of calm and clarity. Here are a few simple meditation techniques to get you started:

1. **Breath Awareness Meditation:**
    - Sit comfortably with your back straight and your hands resting on your lap.
    - Close your eyes and take a few deep breaths.
    - Focus your attention on your breath, noticing the rise and fall of your chest or the sensation of air passing through your nostrils.
    - When your mind wanders, gently bring your focus back to your breath.

2. **Body Scan Meditation:**
   - Lie down or sit comfortably.
   - Close your eyes and take a few deep breaths.
   - Slowly bring your attention to different parts of your body, starting from your toes and moving up to your head.
   - Notice any sensations, tension, or areas of relaxation.
3. **Loving-Kindness Meditation:**
   - Sit comfortably and close your eyes.
   - Take a few deep breaths and bring to mind someone you care about.
   - Silently repeat phrases such as "May you be happy, may you be healthy, may you be safe, may you live with ease."
   - Extend these wishes to yourself and others in your life.

Daily Mindfulness Exercises

Incorporating mindfulness into your daily routine doesn't have to be time-consuming. Here are some simple exercises to practice mindfulness throughout the day:

1. **Mindful Eating:**
    - Slow down and savor each bite.
    - Notice the taste, texture, and aroma of your food.
    - Pay attention to how your body feels as you eat.
2. **Mindful Walking:**
    - Take a walk and focus on the sensation of your feet touching the ground.
    - Notice the sights, sounds, and smells around you.
    - Breathe deeply and enjoy the present moment.
3. **Mindful Listening:**
    - When talking to someone, give them your full attention.
    - Listen without interrupting or planning your response.
    - Notice the tone, pace, and emotions in their voice.
4. **Mindful Breathing:**
    - Take a few moments throughout the day to focus on your breath.

- Inhale deeply through your nose, hold for a few seconds, and exhale slowly through your mouth.
- Repeat this a few times to center yourself.

"The present moment is filled with joy and happiness. If you are attentive, you will see it." – Thich Nhat Hanh

Practicing mindfulness and meditation is a lifelong journey. By integrating these practices into your daily routine, you can cultivate a deeper sense of awareness, reduce stress, and enhance your overall well-being. Remember, it's not about perfection but about making a consistent effort to live more mindfully each day.

Chapter 2: Physical Well-Being

Physical well-being is the foundation of a healthy and fulfilling life. It encompasses everything from nutrition and exercise to rest and relaxation. By taking care of your body, you are not only enhancing your physical health but also boosting your mental and emotional well-being. This chapter explores practical tips and strategies to help you nurture your body and maintain a balanced, healthy lifestyle.

Healthy Eating Habits

Nutrition is a crucial component of physical well-being. A balanced diet provides the energy and nutrients your body needs to function optimally. Here are some tips to help you make healthier food choices:

1. **Eat a Rainbow:** Incorporate a variety of colorful fruits and vegetables into your meals. Each color provides different essential nutrients.
2. **Balanced Meals:** Ensure your meals include a mix of protein, healthy fats, and complex carbohydrates.

3. **Stay Hydrated:** Drink plenty of water throughout the day. Aim for at least eight 8-ounce glasses daily.
4. **Mindful Eating:** Pay attention to your hunger and fullness cues. Eat slowly and savor each bite.
5. **Limit Processed Foods:** Opt for whole, unprocessed foods whenever possible. Reduce your intake of sugar, salt, and unhealthy fats.

Sample Meal Plan:

- **Breakfast:** Greek yogurt with fresh berries and a sprinkle of granola
- **Lunch:** Quinoa salad with mixed greens, chickpeas, avocado, and a lemon-tahini dressing
- **Dinner:** Grilled salmon with roasted sweet potatoes and steamed broccoli
- **Snacks:** Apple slices with almond butter, a handful of nuts, or baby carrots with hummus

Exercise Routines

Regular physical activity is vital for maintaining physical well-being. It strengthens your body, improves cardiovascular health, boosts mood, and enhances overall fitness. Here are some fun and effective workouts for all fitness levels:

1. **Cardio Workouts:**
    - **Walking/Jogging:** Start with brisk walking and gradually increase to jogging.
    - **Dancing:** Join a dance class or follow along with online dance workout videos.
    - **Cycling:** Ride a bike outdoors or use a stationary bike indoors.
2. **Strength Training:**
    - **Bodyweight Exercises:** Include push-ups, squats, lunges, and planks.
    - **Resistance Bands:** Use bands for added resistance in exercises like bicep curls and shoulder presses.
    - **Free Weights:** Incorporate dumbbells or kettlebells into your routine.

3. **Flexibility and Balance:**
   - **Yoga:** Practice yoga to improve flexibility, balance, and mental clarity.
   - **Pilates:** Strengthen your core and enhance body awareness with Pilates exercises.
   - **Stretching:** Incorporate daily stretching routines to maintain flexibility and prevent injury.

Weekly Workout Plan:

- **Monday:** 30 minutes of cardio (walking/jogging) + 20 minutes of strength training (bodyweight exercises)
- **Tuesday:** Yoga session (30 minutes)
- **Wednesday:** 30 minutes of cycling + 20 minutes of strength training (resistance bands)
- **Thursday:** Pilates session (30 minutes)
- **Friday:** 30 minutes of cardio (dancing) + 20 minutes of strength training (free weights)
- **Saturday:** Rest day or gentle stretching
- **Sunday:** Outdoor hike or nature walk (45 minutes)

Rest and Relaxation

Rest and relaxation are just as important as nutrition and exercise in maintaining physical well-being. Quality sleep and restorative practices allow your body to recover and rejuvenate. Here are some tips to help you achieve restful sleep and relaxation:

1. **Establish a Sleep Routine:**
   - Go to bed and wake up at the same time every day, even on weekends.
   - Create a calming bedtime routine, such as reading a book or taking a warm bath.
2. **Create a Sleep-Friendly Environment:**
   - Keep your bedroom cool, dark, and quiet.
   - Invest in a comfortable mattress and pillows.
   - Limit screen time before bed to reduce blue light exposure.
3. **Practice Relaxation Techniques:**
   - **Deep Breathing:** Practice deep breathing exercises to calm your mind and body.

- **Progressive Muscle Relaxation:** Tense and relax different muscle groups to release tension.
- **Meditation:** Incorporate mindfulness or guided meditation before bed to promote relaxation.

Sample Relaxation Routine:

- **Evening:** Enjoy a cup of herbal tea and write in a journal.
- **Before Bed:** Dim the lights and do a gentle stretching routine.
- **In Bed:** Practice deep breathing or listen to a guided meditation.

"Take care of your body. It's the only place you have to live." – Jim Rohn

By incorporating these healthy eating habits, exercise routines, and relaxation techniques into your daily life, you can enhance your physical well-being and enjoy a more vibrant, energetic, and fulfilling lifestyle. Remember, taking care of your body is an act of self-love and a crucial step towards overall wellness.

Chapter 3: Emotional Health

Emotional health is the cornerstone of a balanced and fulfilling life. It involves understanding, managing, and expressing your emotions in a healthy way. Strong emotional health helps you navigate life's challenges, build meaningful relationships, and maintain a positive outlook. This chapter offers practical strategies and insights to help you enhance your emotional well-being.

Understanding Emotions

Emotions are a natural part of the human experience. They provide valuable information about our needs, desires, and responses to the world around us. Understanding your emotions is the first step toward emotional health.

1. **Identify Your Emotions:**
    - Take time to notice and name your feelings. Are you happy, sad, angry, or anxious?
    - Use an emotion wheel to expand your emotional vocabulary and pinpoint specific feelings.

2. **Accept Your Emotions:**
     - Allow yourself to feel emotions without judgment. It's okay to experience a wide range of feelings.
     - Understand that all emotions, even negative ones, serve a purpose and can guide you toward personal growth.
3. **Reflect on Your Emotions:**
     - Consider what triggers certain emotions and how they affect your thoughts and behaviors.
     - Journaling can be a helpful tool for exploring your feelings and gaining insights.

Journaling Prompts

Journaling is a powerful practice for emotional expression and self-reflection. Here are some prompts to help you get started:

1. **Daily Check-In:**
     - How am I feeling right now?
     - What events or thoughts contributed to these feelings?
     -

2. **Exploring Emotions:**
   - Describe a recent emotional experience. What happened, and how did you react?
   - What emotions do I find most challenging to deal with, and why?
3. **Gratitude Journal:**
   - List three things you are grateful for today.
   - How did these positive aspects impact your emotions?
4. **Personal Growth:**
   - What is a recent challenge I faced, and what did I learn from it?
   - How can I better manage my emotions in the future?

Building Resilience

Resilience is the ability to bounce back from adversity and maintain emotional balance. Developing resilience helps you cope with stress and navigate life's ups and downs with greater ease.

1. **Cultivate a Positive Mindset:**
    - Focus on your strengths and past successes. Remind yourself of your ability to overcome challenges.
    - Practice positive affirmations to build self-confidence and optimism.
2. **Develop Healthy Coping Strategies:**
    - Engage in activities that reduce stress and promote relaxation, such as yoga, meditation, or spending time in nature.
    - Talk to someone you trust about your feelings. Sharing your experiences can provide comfort and perspective.
3. **Set Realistic Goals:**
    - Break down larger goals into manageable steps. Celebrate small victories along the way.
    - Be kind to yourself and recognize that setbacks are a natural part of the growth process.

4. **Foster a Supportive Network:**
   - Surround yourself with positive and supportive people who uplift and encourage you.
   - Participate in community activities or join support groups to build connections and find shared understanding.

Practicing Self-Compassion

Self-compassion involves treating yourself with kindness and understanding, especially during times of difficulty. It helps you maintain emotional balance and fosters a healthier relationship with yourself.

1. **Be Kind to Yourself:**
   - Speak to yourself with the same kindness and care you would offer a friend.
   - Acknowledge your efforts and progress, rather than focusing on perceived shortcomings.

2. **Practice Self-Forgiveness:**
   - Let go of self-criticism and forgive yourself for mistakes or imperfections.
   - Understand that everyone makes mistakes and that they are opportunities for growth.
3. **Mindful Self-Compassion:**
   - Incorporate mindfulness practices to stay present and aware of your emotions without judgment.
   - Use self-compassionate phrases, such as "I am doing my best," or "It's okay to feel this way."

"You don't have to control your thoughts. You just have to stop letting them control you."

Dan Millman

Emotional health is an ongoing journey of self-discovery and growth. By understanding your emotions, expressing them healthily, building resilience, and practicing self-compassion, you can enhance your emotional well-being and lead a more balanced, fulfilling life. Remember, emotional health is not about being happy all the time but about embracing the full spectrum of human emotions with grace and understanding.

Chapter 4: Creative Outlets

Creativity is a powerful tool for enhancing emotional well-being and self-expression. Engaging in creative activities allows you to explore your inner world, reduce stress, and find joy in the process of creation. Whether it's through art, writing, music, or other forms of creativity, these outlets can provide a therapeutic escape and a means to connect with yourself on a deeper level. This chapter delves into the benefits of creative outlets and offers practical ideas to incorporate creativity into your daily life.

The Power of Creativity

Creativity isn't just about producing art; it's a way of thinking and seeing the world. It enables you to express emotions, solve problems, and find beauty in the everyday. Here are some key benefits of engaging in creative activities:

1. **Emotional Expression:**
    - Creativity provides a safe space to explore and express complex emotions.

- It can help you process feelings and experiences that are difficult to articulate.

2. **Stress Relief:**
   - Engaging in creative activities can reduce stress and anxiety.
   - It promotes relaxation and mindfulness, allowing you to be fully present in the moment.

3. **Self-Discovery:**
   - Creativity encourages self-exploration and personal growth.
   - It helps you discover new interests, talents, and aspects of your personality.

4. **Enhanced Problem-Solving:**
   - Creative thinking fosters innovation and flexibility.
   - It helps you approach challenges from different perspectives and find unique solutions.

Creative Activities

There are countless ways to incorporate creativity into your life. Here are some ideas to inspire you:

1. **Art:**
   - **Painting and Drawing:** Use watercolors, acrylics, or sketch pencils to create art. Don't worry about perfection; focus on the process.
   - **Crafts:** Try activities like knitting, sewing, or making jewelry. These can be relaxing and rewarding.
   - **Photography:** Capture moments of beauty and create a visual journal of your experiences.
2. **Writing:**
   - **Journaling:** Write about your thoughts, feelings, and daily experiences. Use prompts to spark inspiration.
   - **Creative Writing:** Explore fiction, poetry, or personal essays. Let your imagination run wild.
   - **Blogging:** Share your ideas, stories, or expertise with a wider audience. This can be both fulfilling and community-building.

3. **Music:**
   - **Playing Instruments:** Learn to play an instrument or revisit one you used to play. Music can be a powerful emotional outlet.
   - **Singing:** Sing along to your favorite songs or join a choir. Singing can uplift your mood and build confidence.
   - **Listening to Music:** Create playlists that reflect your emotions or help you relax and unwind.
4. **Movement:**
   - **Dance:** Take a dance class or dance freely at home. Movement can be a joyful and liberating form of expression.
   - **Yoga:** Practice yoga to connect with your body and mind. It combines physical movement with mindfulness.
   - **Theater:** Join a local theater group or participate in improv classes. Acting can be a fun way to explore different aspects of yourself.

Incorporating Creativity into Daily Life

Finding time for creativity can be challenging, but it's worth the effort. Here are some tips to help you make creativity a regular part of your routine:

1. **Schedule Creative Time:**
   - Set aside specific times in your week dedicated to creative activities. Treat it as a non-negotiable appointment with yourself.
2. **Create a Dedicated Space:**
   - Designate a corner of your home as your creative space. Fill it with inspiring materials and tools.
3. **Join a Community:**
   - Participate in creative groups or classes. Being part of a community can provide motivation and support.
4. **Keep it Fun:**
   - Focus on the joy of creation rather than the outcome. Allow yourself to play and experiment without self-judgment.
   -

5. **Combine Creativity with Daily Tasks:**
    - Add creative touches to your everyday life. For example, cook a new recipe, arrange flowers, or decorate your space.

"Creativity is intelligence having fun."

Albert Einstein

Creative outlets are a vital aspect of self-care and emotional well-being. By engaging in artistic and imaginative activities, you can express yourself more fully, reduce stress, and discover new passions. Remember, creativity is not about perfection but about the joy and freedom of expression. Embrace your creative side and let it enrich your life in countless ways.

Chapter 5: Social Connections

Introduction to Social Connections

Human beings are inherently social creatures. Strong social connections are essential for emotional health and overall well-being. Positive relationships provide support, enrich our lives, and contribute to our sense of belonging. This chapter explores the importance of social connections, offers strategies for building and maintaining healthy relationships, and highlights ways to balance self-care with caring for others.

Nurturing Relationships

Healthy relationships are built on trust, communication, and mutual respect. Here are some tips to help you nurture and strengthen your relationships:

1. **Effective Communication:**
    - **Listen Actively:** Give your full attention when someone is speaking. Show empathy and understanding.

- **Express Yourself Clearly:** Share your thoughts and feelings openly and honestly. Use "I" statements to convey your perspective without blaming others.
- **Non-Verbal Communication:** Pay attention to body language, eye contact, and tone of voice. These cues can enhance understanding and connection.

2. **Show Appreciation:**
   - **Express Gratitude:** Regularly acknowledge and appreciate the people in your life. A simple thank you can go a long way.
   - **Acts of Kindness:** Small gestures of kindness, like a thoughtful note or a helping hand, can strengthen bonds.

3. **Spend Quality Time:**
   - **Shared Activities:** Engage in activities you both enjoy. This creates positive experiences and memories.
   - **Regular Check-Ins:** Make time for regular conversations, whether

in person or through phone calls or video chats.
4. **Respect Boundaries:**
    - **Personal Space:** Recognize and respect each other's need for personal space and time alone.
    - **Set Boundaries:** Clearly communicate your own boundaries and be mindful of others'.

The Importance of Community

Belonging to a community provides a sense of connection and support. Whether it's a neighborhood group, a hobby club, or an online forum, being part of a community can enhance your social well-being.

1. **Finding Your Tribe:**
    - **Common Interests:** Join groups or clubs that align with your interests and passions.
    - **Volunteering:** Participate in volunteer activities. It's a great way to meet like-minded people while giving back.
    -

2. **Building a Support Network:**
   - **Reach Out:** Don't hesitate to reach out to others when you need support. True connections are built through vulnerability and mutual care.
   - **Be Supportive:** Offer help and support to those in your community. Acts of kindness and generosity foster deeper connections.
3. **Participating in Community Events:**
   - **Local Events:** Attend local events, such as farmers' markets, festivals, or community meetings. These gatherings provide opportunities to meet new people.
   - **Online Communities:** Join online groups and forums related to your interests. Virtual communities can be just as supportive as physical ones.

Self-Care in Relationships

Balancing self-care with caring for others is crucial. Ensuring your own well-being enables you to be a better friend, partner, or family member.

1. **Prioritize Self-Care:**
    - **Set Boundaries:** Learn to say no when you need to. It's okay to prioritize your well-being.
    - **Regular Self-Check-Ins:** Regularly assess your emotional and physical health. Make adjustments as needed to avoid burnout.
2. **Healthy Balance:**
    - **Time Management:** Allocate time for yourself and your social connections. A balanced schedule can prevent feelings of overwhelm.
    - **Mindful Presence:** When spending time with others, be fully present. Quality interactions are more fulfilling than quantity.
3. **Seek Support When Needed:**
    - **Professional Help:** If you're struggling with maintaining balance or dealing with relationship issues, consider seeking professional help, such as therapy or counseling.

- **Lean on Your Network:** Don't hesitate to lean on your support network when needed. Sharing your burdens can lighten the load.

"Surround yourself with only people who are going to lift you higher." – Oprah Winfrey

Strong social connections are a cornerstone of emotional and physical well-being. By nurturing relationships, participating in communities, and balancing self-care with caring for others, you can build a supportive and fulfilling social network. Remember, meaningful connections enrich your life and provide the support and joy needed to thrive. Embrace the power of relationships and the sense of belonging they bring.

Chapter 6: Self-Love and Acceptance

Introduction to Self-Love and Acceptance

Self-love and acceptance are foundational pillars of personal growth and well-being. Embracing who you are, with all your strengths and imperfections, fosters inner peace, resilience, and a positive outlook on life. This chapter explores the importance of self-love, offers practical strategies to cultivate self-acceptance, and emphasizes the transformative power of treating yourself with compassion and kindness.

Understanding Self-Love

Self-love is the practice of nurturing your own well-being and happiness. It involves recognizing your worth, honoring your needs, and caring for yourself with the same compassion you show others. Here are key aspects of cultivating self-love:

1. **Self-Awareness:**
   - **Know Yourself:** Understand your values, strengths, and areas for

growth. Self-awareness is the foundation of self-love.
- **Embrace Authenticity:** Celebrate your uniqueness and embrace all aspects of your identity, including your quirks and vulnerabilities.

2. **Self-Care Practices:**
   - **Physical Self-Care:** Prioritize activities that nourish your body, such as exercise, nutritious eating, and adequate rest.
   - **Emotional Self-Care:** Engage in activities that promote emotional well-being, such as journaling, mindfulness, and spending time in nature.
   - **Spiritual Self-Care:** Connect with practices that nurture your spirit, whether through meditation, prayer, or engaging in activities that bring you joy.

3. **Setting Boundaries:**
   - **Protect Your Energy:** Learn to say no to activities or relationships that drain your energy or compromise your well-being.

- **Respect Your Limits:** Honor your physical, emotional, and mental limits. Boundaries are essential for self-respect and self-care.

Practicing Self-Acceptance

Self-acceptance is the unconditional acknowledgment and appreciation of who you are, including your strengths, weaknesses, and unique qualities. It involves letting go of self-judgment and embracing self-compassion. Here are strategies to foster self-acceptance:

1. **Challenge Inner Criticism:**
   - **Identify Negative Thoughts:** Notice when self-critical thoughts arise. Challenge them with kindness and rationality.
   - **Practice Affirmations:** Replace self-criticism with positive affirmations that affirm your worth and capabilities.
2. **Cultivate Self-Compassion:**
   - **Be Kind to Yourself:** Treat yourself with the same kindness

and understanding you would offer a loved one facing a challenge.
- **Practice Mindfulness:** Stay present and aware of your thoughts and feelings without judgment. Mindfulness cultivates self-compassion.

3. **Celebrate Your Achievements:**
   - **Acknowledge Successes:** Celebrate your accomplishments, no matter how small. Give yourself credit for your efforts and achievements.
   - **Learn from Setbacks:** View setbacks as opportunities for growth and learning rather than reasons for self-criticism.

4. **Surround Yourself with Positivity:**
   - **Choose Supportive Relationships:** Surround yourself with people who uplift and encourage you. Positive relationships reinforce self-acceptance.
   - **Limit Exposure to Negativity:** Minimize exposure to negative

influences, whether in media, social interactions, or self-talk.
- **Practice Mindfulness:** Stay present and aware of your thoughts and feelings without judgment. Mindfulness cultivates self-compassion.

5. **Celebrate Your Achievements:**
    - **Acknowledge Successes:** Celebrate your accomplishments, no matter how small. Give yourself credit for your efforts and achievements.
    - **Learn from Setbacks:** View setbacks as opportunities for growth and learning rather than reasons for self-criticism.

6. **Surround Yourself with Positivity:**
    - **Choose Supportive Relationships:** Surround yourself with people who uplift and encourage you. Positive relationships reinforce self-acceptance.

- **Limit Exposure to Negativity:** Minimize exposure to negative influences, whether in media, social interactions, or self-talk.

"To love oneself is the beginning of a lifelong romance." – Oscar Wilde

Self-love and acceptance are transformative practices that empower you to live authentically and joyfully. By nurturing self-awareness, practicing self-care, cultivating self-compassion, and embracing imperfection, you can build a foundation of inner strength and resilience. Remember, you are worthy of love and acceptance—beginning with yourself. Embrace your uniqueness and celebrate the journey of self-discovery and growth.

Final Thoughts

As you reach the end of **Nurturing You: A Self-Care Guide for Women**, take a moment to reflect on the journey you have undertaken. This guide was designed to be more than just a book; it's a companion on your path to holistic well-being and self-discovery.

You've explored the various facets of self-care, from mindfulness and meditation to physical well-being, emotional health, creative outlets, social connections, and the vital practice of self-love and acceptance. Each chapter has offered you tools, insights, and practices to help you prioritize and nurture yourself, reinforcing the understanding that self-care is not a one-time act but an ongoing, essential part of life.

As you integrate these practices into your daily routine, remember that self-care is a personal journey. What works for one person might not work for another, and that's okay. The key is to listen to your own needs and honor what feels right for you. This guide has provided a variety of approaches, allowing you to experiment and find the self-care rituals that resonate most deeply with you.

Here are a few final thoughts to carry with you:

- **Consistency is Key**: Regular self-care practices can make a profound difference in your overall well-being. Even small, consistent actions can have a significant impact over time.
- **Be Kind to Yourself**: Self-care is about self-compassion. On days when you find it challenging to make time for yourself, remember that it's okay to start small. Every step you take towards caring for yourself is valuable.
- **Celebrate Your Progress**: Acknowledge and celebrate the strides you've made in your self-care journey. Each act of self-nurturing is a testament to your commitment to your own well-being.
- **Stay Open to Growth**: Your needs and circumstances will evolve over time. Stay open to adapting and growing your self-care practices to align with where you are in your life.

By nurturing yourself, you create a foundation of strength, resilience, and joy that extends into every aspect of your life. You become more capable of supporting others, pursuing your passions, and navigating life's challenges with grace and confidence.

Remember, self-care is not selfish; it is a necessary investment in your health and happiness. You are deserving of the love, care, and attention you give to yourself. Embrace this journey with an open heart and a compassionate spirit, knowing that by nurturing you, you are nurturing the world around you.

Thank you for allowing this guide to be a part of your self-care journey. May you continue to grow, flourish, and live a life filled with love, joy, and well-being.

With warmth and encouragement,

Jennifer L. Baldwin

www.ingramcontent.com/pod-product-compliance
Lightning Source LLC
LaVergne TN
LVHW061623070526
838199LV00078B/7396